Martha's Vineyard

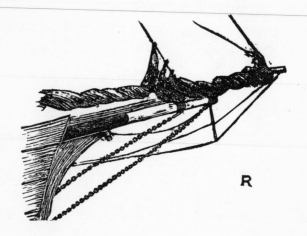

R

POEMS BY
MARION LINEAWEAVER · BARBARA BRADLEY
ROBERT T. HYDE · DIONIS COFFIN RIGGS

MARTHA'S
VINEYARD

BLOCKPRINTS BY SIDNEY NOYES RIGGS

WITH A FOREWORD BY HENRY BEETLE HOUGH

WILLIAM L. BAUHAN, PUBLISHER
DUBLIN · NEW HAMPSHIRE

Contents

Foreword

IT WOULD BE APPROPRIATE for this book of Island poems to have an overture rather than a foreword; this is not to suggest an analogy between the arts, which may or may not exist, but to recognize the qualities of the poems themselves, and the fact that four poets have joined in an orchestration which has not only music but color, fantasy, and a warm pulse of life. Indeed, many readers will have experienced a sort of prelude, if not an overture, in the fragrances, land and sea sounds, and Island-feeling of Martha's Vineyard.

Will such readers find themselves especially privileged, or will the greater reward go to those who are discoverers, like new-comers on a fair shore or a high hill? It is difficult to say; the real point is that although the name "Martha's Vineyard" in the title of the volume — and a beautiful name it has always been — is accurate and suitable, there is no exclusiveness about it. These are Island poems, but they are no more narrowly restricted than the songs of Ariel.

The voices of the four poets are individual and different, yet they seem to belong together naturally rather than by artifice. Which speaks of "the shoreline's rib, the rippled muscular seas;" which beckons along the worn path that leads "over the red-grass fields, beyond the solemn woods;" for which do "October's burly winds and brawny cold hammer the maple leaves to beaten gold;" and which speaks of a "white, curious transfigure-ment, this dear familiar setting after bitter storm?"

There should be no suggestion that these are nature poems only, although they belong to an Island which remains a symbol of eternal nature uncorrupted, and of experience past and present in an evocative natural setting; they penetrate acutely and unobtrusively into matters of mind, spirit, and emotion, and even the specific allusions are suggestive of more than the special circumstances from which they spring.

Let Martha's Vineyard, nevertheless, make a just claim here of something approaching uniqueness in having within its modest realm of village, moor, hill, and shore, four poetic voices such as these, together with an artist whose insight and command of an appropriate medium provide illustrations so closely complementing the words. And what other Island of the New World can show successful realization of the sestina, that twelfth century Provençal form used so long ago by Dante and Petrarch?

HENRY BEETLE HOUGH

Painting of a Coastal Town

No passion here,
No color squandered; space is bound
By a north light harshly shed
On the gaunt rocks,
On the rigid houses
Of the windy town where I was bred.

A black-backed gull
Stabs his triangular note
Through the sky's washed sadness;
His wings beat at my throat
With a rush of gladness
And the austere monotone
Of the background answers to me,
Answers and is my own
With all the strength
My life has ever known:
The shoreline's rib,
The rippled, muscular seas,
These — only these.

MARION LINEAWEAVER

We have come in a still winter noon.
Seaweed streamers, brown, sun-bleached white,
And gray, dotted with shells and brine,
Outline the shore of the salt water pond.
The beach plum bushes, half-buried in the sand,
Show no promise of May.

The worn beachgrass lies yellow-gray
Against the sand. Last summer's primrose stalks
And goldenrod are sketched in shadow
With softer lines than those that stand
Stiffly defying the wind
That may come soon.

A lazy tide picks up small rafts of weed
And moves then gently over the surface,
Making crab-like shadows
On the rippled bottom, where
Scallop shells lie empty, magnified
By the clear water.

Fog lingers near the island shore.
We hear the warning fog-horn
Repeated and repeated. Here
Only the mellowness of mist shows
In the pastel-tinted woods beyond
The still expanse of the pond.

The gulls, that yesterday were screaming
Over the clam flats, are still.

The men have drawn their boats ashore
And made them fast. A dory floats
Doubled in the water;
A rusty derrick is twice red.

The gulls cannot rest long.
We hear them talking together
After their naps, flying in groups,
Calling back, but not eagerly
As in a clear cold day. Their wings
Splash as they lift and fold them.

A hammering echoes over the water.
Wind makes little waves, and rustles
The beachgrass. We roll up seaweed
And carry away armloads, smelling of iodine
And sea. Sand drips through it
And rattles as we walk.

DIONIS COFFIN RIGGS

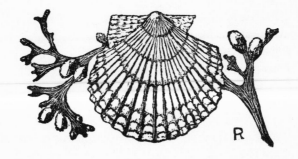

The Barn Owl

We quarrelled, my daughter and I,
Until we were afraid of our native tongue.
Driving home, ground-fog in a treacherous layer
Grazed the grasslands as high as the car.
The headlights were flung
Back like banners.
Four miles never had seemed so far.

When we struck the owl
Still nothing was said. It was dead
When I lifted it, shadow-light,
Talons like exquisite grappling irons
Curled for the catch, and the paradox
Of a heart-shaped face. We spread the wings,
Each taking one, touched their fine grain,
The breast's gossamer down. No wonder an owl
Can skim, drift, float like a flake of smoke . . .

At home we built up a high bright fire.
I had killed; there was nothing to say,
But my daughter fetched on a copper tray
Red wine and mussels, apricot-plump
In their blue shells. We had gathered them early
And now came closer to that harmonious dawn
Than we had been all day.

MARION LINEAWEAVER

NOONTIME

Never before
have I slept
under this small
lilac tree
at noon.

Whether I wake
or stay sleeping
the heart-shaped leaves
dance shadow and sun
on my face.

Never before
have I known
so many blossoms,
so many plumes
of white.

Nor have I heard,
waking or dreaming,
this full chorale
of the bees
and wind.

Why have I
never before seen
the shine on the butter-
cup when I was
sleeping?

DIONIS COFFIN RIGGS

[14]

ESPECIAL SEASON

O was there ever, was there such a May?
Day after crystal day? Such nights of haunted whippoorwill?
Dawns of the catbird's laugh,
mocking at will the towhee, finch and oriole?
Ever a vision of celestial robes
like island dogwood, rose and ivory,
through all the astral shimmer of its bloom?
Ever a newly minted lode of ore
to match the gold assay
of daffodil, forsythia and broom?
Was every tulip quite so gay before?
Every salt breeze so pure?
      Green springs the meadow, for heart and foal.
      Sweetly full swings the lilac, for scent and soul;
      and over, just beyond, promise of summer sea.

Childhood, romance, and age reject the fear
when hope relights, as tangible and sure
as tall horse-chestnut candles lining the village ways,
in this, the prettiest of Mays.

BARBARA BRADLEY

Some who have read my Odyssey have said
There could be no such monster as Charybdis.
So will the scientist and salesman say,
To make the universe easier to believe.

The submarine should prove the facts of this.
Yet, gyrostabilized in his deep day,
What crewman of the *Thresher* could perceive
That an undersea Niagara lay ahead?

And now the capsule roves light-years away,
Submerged in outer deeps none can conceive,
And sends its findings back like a sounding lead.
Will maelstroms of stars tell what truth is?

Forever is your Odyssey. Go weave
New epics of voyages in hope and dread.
Do you suppose no thunderous abyss
Awaits you, or no god to whom to pray?

ROBERT T. HYDE

NIMBUS

Reality? Or illusion,
when candles taper along every harbor?
When the whole world flares with light, light,
around and across a winter sea,
May-changed to turquoise?
    Now, clearly, without confusion,
the universe means no longer bombs, but space;
no longer *Then,* but *When?*
    Hope, mirrored in life's dear lights:
Lighthouse. Light buoy. Christmas lights.
Sequins and lustre. Twinkle. Footlights.
Moon crescent. Sunslant on loved moors,
on a known and ancient oak.
Pearls. The clown's white.
Venus and Sagittarius. Athens. Rome.
Glitter of today's cities, by plane, by night.
Whitecap. Firelight. Lights of home.
Morning on tall golden grasses.
Laughterlight. Skinlight. Eyes, a face . . .
Sunrise again, again.

BARBARA BRADLEY

The stars are white and old above the wind,
Above the ancient waters of the sea,
Above this molded to my feet, this sand
Still cool and clinging since the tinted rain
Cascaded from the legendary bow
That bridged the bay before the sun went down.

Perpetual as the covenant set down
By hand unknown, a message on the wind
To everywhere, the evanescent bow
Repeats the promise sworn upon the sea
By what eternal power made it rain,
That nevermore shall sea submerge the sand.

Most intimate becomes upon the sand
The bond of flesh and earth: as roots go down
In loam, so feet in sand. Then let the rain
Feed growth and love like manna on the wind,
To nourish life and not a waste of sea,
For such has been the promise of the bow.

The arch of colors in the sunlit bow
Had meaning when it curved above the sand,
But what above a never-ending sea?
What need of rainbows if the sun is down
Forever on a nothingness of wind
And darkness, death, and everlasting rain?

Purpose and promise there must be in rain
Illuminated by the sun, whose bow

Requires an admiration that the wind
And ocean cannot quench, a love of sand
Which gives a place to stand upon, put down
The feet affectionately beside the sea.

The waters shall not rise again, the sea
To overwhelm the love of life with rain;
But neither shall the soul of man look down
Forgetful that the promise of the bow
Which set his feet so gently in the sand
Includes as well the stars above the wind.

Sea-promise keep there, covenant and bow,
Rain-fed and nourished man upon the sand,
Down by the shore of stars, blessing the wind.

ROBERT T. HYDE

THE HAVEN

Morning harbor:

At each mooring
Boats reflected
And very still:

The ferry horn
　Ruffles the air,

And ripples go
To rock the yachts
　From everywhere.

ROBERT T. HYDE

UP ISLAND

Three walk in the wind,
wind of young April.
Hear how a pheasant cries,
deep in the brake.
Feel how new strength of sun
melts countryroad tar underfoot.
See, on a remote hill
a muted blur
of soft, greenpromise pinks.
Smell mud and hen and farm
and black young bulls in a field.
Under tall bladeblue skies
the willows make
gold where icebrooklets run.
The beaches stand
cleanswept and waiting.
The sea still holds
its fierce blue wintry sweep:
bold blue of Viking eyes.

Brisk, softheeled steps; all silent.

Speech must not stir
this fragile wine of days
spilling lipchill, heartwarm
from bottles, wintersealed.

Three walk in the wind,
wind of young April.

BARBARA BRADLEY

Dwell in the deeper senses, one by one,
Those arteries of poetry, the source
Of stars and forests, flowers, diamonds, tides.
Balance: the tilting marsh-hawk on the air,
Dark master of the winds, or ships that turn
Their smooth, exact sides to the sea's power

Perpetually offering that power
The contours that make hull and water one.
Both are the heart of rhythm, like the turn
Of rounding seasons. Rhythm: the ruby source
Of passionate love, or horns on pastoral air
Winding their melody above harmonic tides.

Delicate, thin-winged thrushes follow tides
That sweep, with an invisibly walled power,
Migrating flocks to Carribean air,
Guided by constellations. Is there one
Who knows not in his intricate bones the source
Which in the vast night navigates the turn?

When the first man took shape, and in her turn
Woman broke from his rib, then did the tides
Of time unlock the future and the source.
Light overtook light, accumulating power
Year after million years, each teeming one
Enriching and refreshing the world's air.

And yet how narrow is our shroud of air —
A few miles; nothing more than a single turn

Of a single mind can fly from. Praised be the one
Magnificent human dream, whose youthful tides
Engulf the galaxies, whose ancient power
Is the result of courage, and the source.

What flash of metaphor reveals the source
Of earth, volcanic fire, water and air
To be the same? Insight: the balanced power
Of rhythm and direction, that can turn
Time and space back and stem their noble tides,
Relate their pattern to the absolute one.

Senses, the source of living, are in turn
Diaphanous as air, changing as tides,
Kingdom of power and glory of the One.

MARION LINEAWEAVER

The Clamdigger

Louisa, when I offered
To dig up huckleberry bushes
From the swamp
And plant them in your garden
You said no,
You'd risk the sunstroke,
Poison ivy, poison oak,
Just for the sake
Of picking berries in the pasture
Where you could hear the chickadees
Call from the nearby woods,
The scratching of chewinks
In dead brown leaves and sticks;
Or see a striped quail whir up
From her hidden chicks.

By the same token, Louisa,
I would go to Squibnocket for quahaugs,
And wade thigh-deep
In the cold, green water of the creek
That slaps against my boots
And trickles in.
(Don't tell me I'll catch cold!)
I'd feel the clink of hard shells
On my rake, the heft
Of quahaugs in my hand.
I'd smell the wild grapes blooming,
And hear the sea gulls mewing
And the upland plover whistling beyond
The wild-rose edges of the pond.

DIONIS COFFIN RIGGS

[24]

Flotsam

Island, poet, each surrounded
By a universe, unbounded:
All the world flows into you,
Crossing over, coming true,
A purpose in the drifting wind,
Beaching gently on the mind.

ROBERT T. HYDE

THE HAMMOCK

Without lifting my head
I can look at a barn, a red cow
And the round eye of a pond.
Where I lie in my hammock
The many-fingered wind
Plucks from the glass chime
A minnikin music of no complexity.
In my mouth is a shred of clover
Whose morsel of honey
Is just enough. One finger
Suffices to push myself
Into the sun that makes me sneeze,
Like pepper; then
Back to the shade
Of the lilac verandah
I solemnly swing
And want not for anything.

MARION LINEAWEAVER

BLUE CLAW

Through amber creek-water
A crab moves cautiously,
One blue claw held at the guard,
Swimmerets fluttering,
Mandibles nibbling,
Pointed legs stepping
On the moss-greened stones.

Then through the taut
Mirror-glaze of his sky
A net splashes, and dips.

DIONIS COFFIN RIGGS

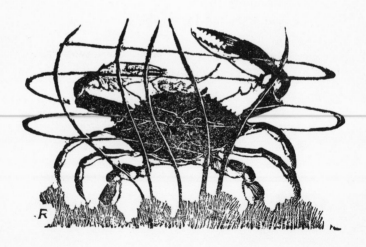

POACHING

Oh but the night's thick
And the inlet slick
As oil under the fog.
There's no sound only a frog
And the oars' muffled click
Skirting the bog.

Here's the stake and the line,
Your work and mine,
Hid well in the salt grass,
Leading to the submerged mass
Of the net and the murky shine
Of striped bass.

The hauling's easy for two,
The pair of us, me and you.
Now for the open hatch,
The struck, tremulous match
Flaring silver and blue
Over our catch.

MARION LINEAWEAVER

I can remember
The clean warm kitchen
With baskets packed
And ready on the table
And grandmother:
    "Come, James,
    Harness the horse.
    The girls are ready
    And the food is packed.
    Eliza and her three boys
    Have just gone up the lane.
    They'll get to Quansoo
    Ahead of us."
        "Let them go.
        They'll open the gate, so
        All we'll have to do is close it
        And make it fast. Are you sure
        You've got everything, Mary?"

The road was rutted, and the sand
Made scratchy noises on the wheels,
The scrub oaks brushed the carriage sides.
Grandpa sang sea-chanties as soon
As we drew nearer to the sea.
    "What did I tell you?
    They've opened the gate."
        "Let me close it,
        Grandpa!" "Me!" "ME!"
    "Now be little ladies — all three!"

The ocean sounded close,
A rhythmic rumbling beyond the dunes.
The horse laid back his ears,
But grandpa sang his sea-tunes
All the louder.
    "I'll be glad
    To have a dip
    In the surf."
  "James, I'm afraid
  I haven't brought
  Your bathing-suit."
    "I asked you, Mary,
    If you had everything."
  "I have the children's suits
  And mine — but
  I couldn't find yours, James.
  Besides, you never swim."
    "But I like
    To go into the water.
    What else have you forgotten?"
  "I've got the chicken,
  Bread and butter,
  Hard-cooked eggs — "
    "Salt and pepper?"
  "Yes, salt and pepper
  In little twists of paper.
  Bananas, cookies — "
    "Anything to drink?"
  "A whole gallon of lemonade.
  We'll bury it in the sand
  To keep it cool."
    "It seems as if
    You might have brought
    My bathing-suit."

"No one will mind
If you go bathing
In your underwear."
  "My underwear!
  I never heard of doing
  Such a thing!"

The sand was hot on our bare feet,
The wind came from the sun-warmed land
Smelling of sweet-fern, bay, and oak.
It pushed back the breakers into rolls
Of white-tipped green.
The boys made forts at the sea's edge
And the girls houses with pebbled paths,
And gardens of dry rockweed.
  "Come, get your sun-bonnets,
  Little dears. Boys, get your caps,
  You'll be as red as lobsters."
      "May we put on
      Our bathing-suits,
      Grandma?"
"Yes, the tide is right
For a swim. Sometimes
The waves are much too strong.
Now we can ride those combers
As though they were green horses."
      "Grandma, how old were you
      When you learned how to swim?"
"No bigger than you.
We grew up swimming
In Sydney Harbor."

"Why didn't grandpa
Learn to swim? You'd think
With water all around — "
"And being a sea-captain — "
"He always thought it was quicker
To sail a boat. But he likes
To go into the water.
James, suppose you wear my suit?"
    "I'd look fine — six-foot-one
    In a bathing-suit of yours!"
"It's loose, and has long legs.
You needn't use the skirt."
        "Grandpa's going into the water
        In grandma's bathing-suit,
        Bathing-suit, bathing-suit — "
"Keep still, the pack of you,
Or I shan't go in at all."

A barn stood midway between the bridge
Over the creek and the opening
That let the water go
From Tisbury Great Pond into the sea.
It was our bath-house now.
Grandpa and the boys used the horses' stalls
And came out soon
In bathing-suits instead of overalls.
        "You don't look too bad, grandpa,
        Except you've got it on backwards."
    "What's the odds? 'Twill do
    For a dip in the surf."
The girls went next
And grandma helped to cover us
With cream against the sun and wind.

"Have a good time, but stay
On the sandbar. Come ashore
If you feel the undertow,
And don't go out too far."

We ran down to the sea
And screamed as the water
Touched toe and leg and knee.
We ran in and got wet all over.
We played like seals in the breakers,
Jumping through and through the combers.
Grandpa, like a big walrus, played too.
    "Come on now, we'll go ashore,
    It's getting rough.
    Take hands, each one,
    Hold tight in a long line."

Then he saw grandma
Pull off her heavy cotton skirt,
Her petticoats, her long-sleeved waist,
And run into the water, swimming past —
    "What in thunder — "
Why, one was missing from the line.
How small it must have looked to him,
That line, with one child
Gone!
He led five children to the shallows
And turned back.
    "I'm coming, Mary."

She pulled me by the long dark braids
And swam, dragging me after her
To the place where grandpa stood
Rocklike, reaching toward us.

He didn't look at me
But took grandma in his arms.
I clung to them as best I could.
  "Come, I'll take you home."
  "Of course not, James.
  We'll go right on with the picnic."

I can remember
Aunt Eliza offering me
Her choicest cookies, and the boys
Looking wonderingly, as though
I'd been on a long adventurous journey.
They were quiet all the afternoon.

I can feel the drowsiness,
The comfort of grandmother's arms,
And the steady jog, jog
Of the horse's hoofs
On the way home.

DIONIS COFFIN RIGGS

THE SUMMER GIRLS

Fog this winter is thick as flannel.
The waterfront is an ice-bound wall.
The lighthouse looms by the frozen channel.
Do you remember summer at all?

June days like a chain of amber,
Thirty nights like black pearls;
To the streets of town came the summer girls,
Their dresses swinging, their eyes singing.

Music, music of dancing skirts,
The flash of brown legs, voices blowing
Over the water from shadowy decks
And the moon in full bloom, gold and glowing.

The bell clanged in the fiery dawn
Waking us to a sailor's warning;
The girls leaned on their window-sills
And laughed into the face of morning.

They laughed and loved and swam in July
In the shallow sea like a sheet of flowers.
We found on the dunes where we used to meet
The fleeting prints of their narrow feet.

When the bell rang in the August rain
And mackerel gulls were a scatter of white
Rumor of wind came back again,
Promise of storm for an autumn night.

The girls danced on the Yacht Club lawn
And we watched them over the picket fence,
Standing our ground; but they took our measure;
We said, "The summer will soon be gone."

Do you remember the fog bell
And hoping the storm would break at last?
The visiting yachts had left the harbor,
Our own boats were all made fast.

The girls drifted their inland ways
With the sapphire days of early September.
Murmurous ruin swelled in the surf,
Dusty mist rolled over the moors

And we rode on the dripping elastic turf
And fished and hunted and walked the town
In the silent evenings. The summer houses
Were locked and bolted with blinds drawn.

When the gale slammed its ponderous door
On Indian Summer the fog bell measured
November, December. The town was ours
And we had whatever it was we treasured . . .

The hanging fog is an icy smother,
No need for the lighthouse bell.
The harbor is peopled with winter moorings,
The town is bare as a hollow shell.

Or do you remember the white blouses,
The warm lips and the blossomy scent
Of the summer girls, with arms bare
And careless glances and yellow hair?

                              MARION LINEAWEAVER

Cumbs, itcometh
Slow to the creeplick fire.
      (Low brighthot firespokes in seawind.)
To the dungarpanted pigheap,
Surfloggered sleepappy peoples
Sproddled in cholly dork sonds,
      Slooooow comes a fingerthin figure,
Spectreyes seakin.
      (Salmonmoon staredown,
Face of a faceless dame, pinkaloframed.)
Who is it? Man is it? You it is,
Me seeking.
Yetchua dead as the sea-age past.
Day mortchuy kneel ni ci Bon'm.
Ye canna find me, hear.

You. You. You. You.
In the milkfoam wavecrash.
In charcoalthreaded shrimpcrawl sands.
      (Lilycups lilycups sandwiches oranges
      Bananas in the basket, in mentibus bananas.)
No need to yoohoo. You. You dominote
Lewdlaff loudlaugh joke ho ho.
Hee hee martini
Ho ho holdfashioned
Chugfulla rum! Ahrum! Aaaahhhrummmmm!
      Nebulous nimbulous westerling oriflamme,
Verdigreen mooncloud, bitterdam nightwind.
Sweatercoats, shoeson, lipstick and huddle.)
      You in you frail you starsprinkle you.

Solosong, chorusong,
Choruslow, hyasweet.
Darkheapit pigglepiles
Chuchutant, shush shush ssshhh.
Blankets and bodies, hampily bundled.
    Me, iam cumbered and saphe
Save for a feastghost fireflicker wanderer,
Sadsea king, seeking.

BARBARA BRADLEY

The Widow

Yes, Nahum always said
The view was pretty from this spot.
He'd sit here by the window, looking out,
Watching the snowflakes hurry
Through the valley to settle on the bare
Brown twigs, and then fill up
Each little cup
Of evening primrose seed.
    You wouldn't be here in the winter?

Nahum thought somewhat
Of putting in a pump,
Then he said he guessed not.
If he didn't have to go
To the foot of the hill for water
He wouldn't see the daffodils
Start green, and then turn gold,
With little caps of snow
If it should come up cold.
    You won't be here in spring?

We always used the kerosene.
Nahum said there's no better light
If the wicks are trimmed
And the chimneys clean.
Electricity fails in these autumn gales.
    You won't be here in fall?
You'd miss the huckleberry turning red
And laid like patchwork over the hills;
You'd miss the goldenrod and asters.

You couldn't pick the beach plums
Or smell the wild grapes ripening.

You'd be here only in the summer!
I'd thought of getting me a little place
In town where I could see more folks
And have things warm and easy.
But now I've changed my mind.
This property is not for sale.
Nahum wouldn't want his house
To stand here lonely, winter, spring,
And fall.

DIONIS COFFIN RIGGS

Come rain, come summer, through the wide old doors,
the island children flock to carrousel.
Remember last year? And the years before?
Remember the starting and the stopping bells?
Scarred spike-browed mustangs, black, flaring in pairs;
eagle-beaked arm, gold rings, a prickly fear
for tanned young parents to encircle there.
    Three generations round out fifty years
of brave striped jerseys filled with chests on edge,
and rapt small faces of all sunbrown shades,
as darkly curly and blown golden heads
revolve to musics changing with the age.

How old are the Flying Horses? Who knows?
How old, a child's heart? Around, around it goes.

BARBARA BRADLEY

FOURTH OF JULY

There should always be
Little boys and girls
Sitting on the porch rail
Like swallows on a wire,
Waiting
To see giant chrysanthemums
Blossom in the sky.

The grown-ups
In wicker chairs admire
The afterglow of sunset,
The brightness of white boats
Moving on the rippled water,
Houses, twice-shining
From the town
Across the harbor.

A burst of light:
Golden, red,
Green, purple, blue,
In stars, in whorls,
In spirals.
Shouts and squeals
From the porch rails;
Lemonade spills.

The children, sunburned
After the picnic,
Chilled by night
And the excitement,

One by one, have turned
From the noise
And the shower of sparks
To sit in grandmother-laps,
To be cuddled by mothers
And wrapped, two in a coat.

Before the quiet sky
Wins back its own
Bright stars,
The children are asleep.

DIONIS COFFIN RIGGS

ILLUMINATION NIGHT: OAK BLUFFS

Just once each year
I can recapture something
Of childhood's summer-scented magic
When, on Illumination Night,
The band plays in the park.
And one by one, instead of stars,
The Chinese lanterns light the dark
Tree-sheltered sky.
The shadows of the oak trees, dwarfed
And twisted by the wind,
Loom giantlike among
The little houses made of wood,
Or gingerbread.
At last each house is hung
From porch to peak
With lanterns, and the people
Sit in rocking chairs, or walk
Around, around the circle.
Wind-stirred sea air,
Marigolds and popcorn,
The smoke of candle wicks.
How brief the flame!

DIONIS COFFIN RIGGS

Leaving Home

Don't leave a shred of the years.
Yes, yes! Strip the house bare
Of hawk nest and lucky-stone;
    Only we care
For arrowheads, chestnuts, the bone
    We dug in the yard.
    I hated the bone;
I remember my frightened tears.

Let the house chill to the sound
Of an empty wind. We have and will hold
Our futile belongings, to kill
    Time growing old,
For ah, they are dear to us still,
    The childhood gods —
    All but the bone.
The bone belongs to the ground.

MARION LINEAWEAVER

DIVORCE

Today I bought
bathingsuits for you,
and found, I thought,
the perfect two.

One green, clear, cold,
like the sea, my pair;
one gold, pale gold,
like your sunbleached hair.

But without me
you will play and swim
by sand and sea.
You will be with him.

BARBARA BRADLEY

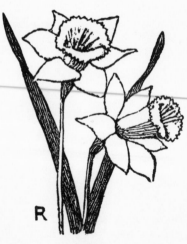

THE BLUE GLASS PEBBLE

I was ten
When I plucked the pebble
From among shell buds,
Rubble and round studs
Of embedded stone.
In my curious hand
It seemed like the eye of God,
In church terrible,
Glaring in furious glass,
But here my own.

I carried it for years
In my warm pocket
That it might be hid,
Yet all the time,
No matter what I did
I knew that it could see.
My talisman, my touchstone!
Its loss is the loss of a friend
And I shall have no watcher at the end
To comfort me.

MARION LINEAWEAVER

'Twas autumn on the seacoast farm
And harvest time was come,
So they stocked up with fish and grain,
Potatoes, fruit, and rum.

With joy the captain's wife hailed in
December, cold and wet:
Her husband soon was promised home
Who had not failed her yet.

The day at last with bright new snow
Stood in the sunrise gleam;
Already was the turkey stuffed,
The pudding on to steam.

Behind her now the table stood
With shining heirlooms set,
But out the window long she gazed
Until her cheeks were wet.

She wondered at the waning day
And thought of things to blame,
But days and weeks and months went by
And still no captain came.

"It could not be the ice," she said,
"It must have been the sea,
For had the ship been frozen in
'Twould long since have been free."

So ended day and ended year
And came the second spring:
The days were warm, the farm was ploughed,
And green on everything.

The captain's wife went through the field
Up to the woodlot bound

And somewhere there dug something green
As green as could be found.

At home again she set it out
Where passers-by could see —
The letters of the captain's name
All planted cleverly.

And every spring the captain's name
Grew up and flourished there,
And in the fall its color stayed
Long after else was bare.

From her lonely bed the captain's wife
Could see her husband's name,
And she wept for him the day she died:
The captain never came.

Successors to the little farm
All turned their ploughs aside;
For years they knew this memory
And proudly let it bide.

At last a stranger bought the place,
Who did not know the tale,
And over all he drove his plough
And flung seed from his pail.

But when the seed came springing up,
The other sprouted too:
In brightest green the people saw
The captain's name anew.

Though many ploughs year after year
Carved furrows on the hill,
Yet to this day the captain's name
In green is seen there still.

ROBERT T. HYDE

WHOSE IS THE LITTLE BOAT?

Whose is the little boat
Anchored in the cove,
A sailboat loved and painted blue
And hidden in the reeds?

Off-islanders have gone,
Their big white cruisers
Drawn up on the shore
And covered.
The fishermen are fishing
With their oilskins on.
The little boat is bobbing,
Ducking, dancing,
In the cattail reeds.
Who lives nearby that needs
This dainty thing?

The worn path leads
Over the red-grass fields,
Beyond the solemn woods,
And there a farm boy rides
His harvester, and turns
To watch the clean grain
Fall behind him in neat rows,
Like waves that splash and dance
Against a painted prow, that lap
A curving gunwale as they spread
And fall astern, like bright waves
With the sunlight shining on them.

DIONIS COFFIN RIGGS

AUTUMNAL

Like sacred towers the cumulus vapor loomed
Commanding over warm blue plains of sky.
We knew the sunlit laughter of July
And vibrant voices when the thunder boomed
Like surf beyond the dunes where ramblers bloomed.
We watched the multicolored butterfly
Pursue its careless flight, and you and I
Forgot that summertime would be consumed.

But now along the byways, hills, and bluffs,
October's burly winds and brawny cold
Hammer the maple leaves to beaten gold
That flares against the sea-blue sky in puffs
Of fabricated flame. And now how soon
We'll walk on white beneath a winter moon.

ROBERT T. HYDE

September Island

Wild grapes
Grow on our island,
Climbing the oak trees,
Lying on flat rocks,
Clambering over stone walls.

We find them in clusters,
Necklaces of opals and rubies
Where they hang from the trees
In the sun; a handful of sapphires
Among the lichens on the stone wall.

We fill our baskets
And sit in the sun.
Fragrance surrounds us —
Sun-warmed bayberry, sweetfern, pine, oak —
As the sun encircles our island.

We do not hurry home, we do not talk,
We sit in the sun and listen
To the sleepy hum of the ocean.
A blue jay calls.
The woodbine is turning red.

DIONIS COFFIN RIGGS

Resort Town

Those ancient summer houses hump
like elephants along the shore,
each a grotesque amorphous lump
for fourscore weathered years and more.
Like elephants along the shore,
the trunk line stands: impassive, gray
for fourscore weathered years and more,
through hurricane, through halcyon day.
The trunk line stands: impassive, gray.

I watch the houses age with me,
through hurricane, through halcyon day.
Battered by gale and memory,
I watch the houses age with me
in lives of storm, half-sea, half-land.
Battered by gale and memory,
sunwarmed and wrinkled, we still stand.

BARBARA BRADLEY

THE STONE SKY

Blown-out November passes. The stacked grasses
Packed in the dunes with webbed and withering roots
Whistle, and spin the pellets of their fruits
On the scoured sand. The chilled toad is gone,
The last grasshopper killed.
Back of the brackish cove huddle clumped rushes
And bay bushes lumped with granular berries.
The air smells of caves; closed is the stone sky.
Beach plum stands black and charred
Against the ancient moor whose sedgey floor
Gathers the dark and hoards it,
Offering no mark to walk by, no sound
But the quawk's guttural bark.

MARION LINEAWEAVER

MULCH

Fall, leaves, fall,
And may the bitter hours drop with you
To the ground.

Cover them all —
That much your musty robes might do
Since you abound.

Rot into dust
Beneath a soft white winter peace
To make new wood.

Regrets may rust,
And bright new energies release,
Perhaps for good.

ROBERT T. HYDE

HER KEY IS MINOR

The face of my delight is tinged with sorrow.
She and the wind possess the empty shores
When winter comes. Then darkly in my marrow
I long for solitude and somber hours.

She and the wind possess the empty shores;
Her time is dusk, her place the wave's grey chasm.
I long for solitude and somber hours,
Watching the surf burst into crumbling blossom.

Her time is dusk, her place the wave's grey chasm;
Her key is minor like the plover's chime.
Watching the surf burst into crumbling blossom
I recognize my mistress and my home.

Her key is minor like the plover's chime.
When winter comes then darkly in my marrow
I recognize my mistress and my home.
The face of my delight is tinged with sorrow.

MARION LINEAWEAVER

THE MAINMAST

In the woods of Mount Katahdin the Maine pine grew,
A seedling sheltered in a lullaby
Strummed where stray sunshine sifted from the sky
And danced to wild tunes the fragrant breezes blew.
Then tall and strong the tapered bole came true,
Swinging aloft its needled galaxy
As if Paul Bunyan waved his broom on high
To sweep the clouds of Androscoggin dew.

Still reaching toward the stars, the pine tree now
Swayed like a mainmast where the night wind plays
A wandering melody upon the stays:
Afloat at last, with yard in place of bough,
The pine fulfilled its Vineyard destiny
To drive an Island ship across the sea.

So outward bound and bending every sail,
Going as graceful as the wind was free,
The clipper rode as tall as any tree
To climb sea mountains with the ponderous whale;
And when her masts were stripped to meet the gale,
All wet and shining in a dance of three
They orbited stiffly in a wooden spree
Like giants in a forest fairy tale.

The voyages of the Mount Katahdin pine
Have carried it around a changing world
And back; and now the faded sails are furled
Forever in a miniature shrine
Memorial of the very tree itself,
Carved in my Vineyard clipper on the shelf.

ROBERT T. HYDE

My sister
Used to tell me
Of the tiger

That sprang
From the wood
And leapt

At a beautiful maiden
Who was waiting
At the edge of the wood,

Awaiting her lover,
Not suspecting
That a tiger

Lurked
In the gray-lichened
Oak wood

Where bracken
And blueberry grew
In the underbrush.

But there
At the edge of the wood
Was the proof:

Two gray
Half-fallen trees,
Caught in each other's

Dead branches,
Trapped in the toils
Of the greenbrier,

Made a terrified
Girl,
And a tiger.

DIONIS COFFIN RIGGS

Migration of Eels

The night must be November,
Rain steady,
Wind nothing.
Stand on the humped whaleback
Of a sand ridge between ocean
And freshwater pond;
Listen:

The skin of the pond splits
And the sound of what it concealed
Is a mysterious raking
Of the marram grass,
A hiss of the blades.
The dark chokes
With a metallic reek;
Then like a wall
Rises the nation of eels.

Layers high,
Wide as the vision's disk,
They spill on the beach,
A river of nerves, braiding of muscle,
Grunting of bone. In a breath's take
They gain the sea and are gone.

They will all die
Only to reappear, in rain,
When wind is nothing
At the same time of year,
To follow the mound
Of their black wave yet once more
Until the last tide
Ebbs on the last shore.

MARION LINEAWEAVER

[64]

SEED CATALOGUE

Leaving my desk I stare
Out at the bundled bushes,
Mounds of seaweed, brown burlap.
The garden is gaunt, grotesque.
The gnarled barberry hedge
Rattles its pinchbeck ware.

I shall draw the curtains
And lose myself in the book
While flowers of my dream unfold:
Velvet swarming of pansies,
Peonies, wind-shaken,
And fragrant hyacinths
Intricately scrolled.

MARION LINEAWEAVER

Empty Season

What is left now, November, in the town,
the dear small town of summer's fickle joys?
Only clean-angled rooftops; men and boys
with curls, checked shirts, the seaman's mock-fierce frown;
babies with huge brown eyes staring toward sea;
a barren sidewalk and a dearth of cars;
a few familiar faces in the bars,
eyes out for strangers to monotony;
close-mouthed, since all have lived but don't say how,
with sea and draggers and blue crystal air.
See: all the neat white houses slumber there.
Tomorrow will do just as well as now.
  But sandaled summer ghosts should glide their· feet
  less close behind me in the empty street.

Strange, how these ghostly, rimeswathed piles recall
the lounging, terrycovered suntanned form,
summery, languid, laughing, short and tall.

White, curious transfigurement: this dear
familiar setting after bitter storm.
Weird, how this pattered, splintery sunwarmed pier,
battered by winter violence, still seems warm.

BARBARA BRADLEY

The Planting

Last fall,
Down on my knees,
I dug holes, put in bone meal,
And planted the bulbs,
Points up.

No one was there,
No one, that is, except the cow,
Straining at her tether
Until the drooled-on leather
Stretched, to see what I was doing.

And some of the hens
Had squeezed under the fence.
They lifted their yellow feet,
Tensing the tendons in them,
Looking cornerwise at me.

I kept on digging, planting,
Feeling the warm sun on my back,
Listening to the hens' talk,
And forgot I had to hurry
Or Miriam would be home from church.

First thing I knew she stood there,
"What are you doing, Dan?"
"Oh, nothing much," I said.
But now that she is dead
I'm glad she caught me then

And saw with earthly eyes
I'd planted tulips for her
Where she could have watched them
From the kitchen window
If she'd stayed.

DIONIS COFFIN RIGGS

[69]

Edge of the Marsh

The coldest sound known to the world exists
In the dry rattle of these gawky reeds.
Caught in lumped ice a sodden rowboat lists
At the mercy of winter. Showers of frozen seeds
Pepper the cockpit where a humped gull feeds,
Its lacquered eyeballs hard as yellow beads.
A flight of canvas-back revolves and twists,
Black, like a bull-whip in the fuming mists.

MARION LINEAWEAVER

OMENS

Upon what logic, stranger, dare we base
frailest assumption of security
in rare encounter with a mind, a face
and heart, too foreign yet for surety?
    The way lies murky, through a world of night;
still, in our darkness, all our path runs straight.
The lantern's flicker casts a radiant light,
and we have time to linger, weigh, and wait.

As ice and fireside, sleds and Christmas live
in penetrance of late September chill;
as one mild wind, one spark of crocus give
assurance of wild roses on the hill;
so may a word, a touch, reveal the whole,
in sure, unreasoned presage of the goal.

BARBARA BRADLEY

The Skin Game

My apple tree is stuffed with yellow birds!
A splendid sight against new-falling snow.
      (Their habits, all too villainous for words;
      Free-loading beauties, evil types we know.)

Incredible! The black, the white, the gold!
On every branch they twitter, perch and hover.
      (Female or male, bickering, plump and bold;
      Another book belied by lightsome cover.)

But one must satisfy the winter need
Of well-named grosbeaks: gorgeous avian pigs.
      (Hundreds! A dream come true! Scatter the seed!
      For golden lumps of heaven on bare twigs.)

BARBARA BRADLEY

Winter Dreams

Under the westward slanting sun
    Each rounded hill
    Snowbound and still
Dreams of old summers and future springs,

How the melted snow will sparkle and run
    And the slumbering trees
    From their winter freeze
Will awake at the whisper of brilliant wings.

ROBERT T. HYDE

BIRD WALK

Ernest
Led us over fences
And through meadows.
In his pocket
He kept a key that opened
The private gate.

Ernest
Had the most powerful
Binoculars, and a whistle
That made the sleeping owl
Wake up and blink
In the sunlight.

Ernest
Could tell a red-tailed hawk
From a sharp-shin, in flight.
He could hear the voice
Of a golden plover,
Or a killdeer's note.

But I
Saw the scarlet tanager
Against a blue sky,
Clara saw it hiding
In the lilac bush,
Ernest didn't see it at all.

DIONIS COFFIN RIGGS

No, never shall there be a fall of snow
Again, nor any secret running brook
Reflecting wise delight or laugh or look,
Nor birches swung to learn what children know;
Nor shall the ancient boulders of a wall
Enclose the hidden meaning of a farm,
The loneliness, the privacy, the charm,
The substance of sensation of it all;
Nor shall a shaggy poetry unfold
In subtle melodies the wry surprise,
The simple statement, or the sly surmise
That somehow management has been controlled:
No, never again shall these be found or lost
Without a memory or a touch of Frost.

ROBERT T. HYDE

Stone Wall on a Wooded Hill

Was there no woman here
To plant a lilac bush?
No one to throw a broken bit
Of willowware into the hollow?
Why should a man, alone,
Build on this rocky hill
And labor to fit stone on stone?

If he tamed this wooded place
Why did he go
And leave no trace
Except a piece of wall
Where moss and ferns have grown
And oaks with thin brown roots
Have split the stone?

DIONIS COFFIN RIGGS

Acknowledgments

The authors wish to express their appreciation for permission to reprint in this volume poems which first appeared in the following publications:

BARBARA BRADLEY: *Especial Season, Merrygoround, Resort Town, Wintertwist,* The Vineyard Gazette. *South Beach Picnic,* City Lights, Cleveland, Ohio.

ROBERT T. HYDE: *Autumnal,* Bowdoin Quill.

MARION LINEAWEAVER: *The Barn Owl,* Harper's Magazine. *The Hammock, The Stone Sky, Edge of the Marsh, Blue Glass Pebble,* copyright 1963, 1964 The New York Times. *Painting of a Coastal Town, Her Key is Minor,* copyright 1964, 1965 The Christian Science Monitor. *The Summer Girls,* The Ladies' Home Journal, copyright by the Curtis Publishing Co. *Seed Catalogue,* The Georgia Review. *Migration of Eels,* The New York Herald-Tribune. *Leaving Home,* New-England Galaxy. *Sestina Sensuous,* The Vineyard Gazette. *Painting of a Coastal Town* was awarded the Jane Judge Memorial Prize, Poetry Society of Georgia, 1963; and *Sestina Sensuous* received the James Joyce Award, Poetry Society of America, 1965.

DIONIS COFFIN RIGGS: *Noontime, Fourth of July, September Island, Birdwalk,* copyright 1963, 1964 The Christian Science Monitor. *Gathering Seaweed,* The Minnesota Review. *Sculpture in Oak, Stone Wall on a Wooded Hill, Blue Claw,* The Vineyard Gazette. *The Clamdigger, Illumination Night, The Widow, Whose is the Little Boat?,* The Ladies' Home Journal, copyright 1963 by the Curtis Publishing Co.